D1065060

an invitation to
QUIET

an invitation to
QUIET

EDITED BY
WYNN WHELDON

MQP

Such sights as youthful poets dream
On summer eves by haunted stream.

John Milton

Right after a snowslide comes the most perfect silence. Complete, total silence. You lose almost all sense of where you are.

Haruki Murakami

The height
of power
in women
rests in
tranquillity.

Marquise de Maintenon

What is this life if, full of care,
We have no time to stand and stare.

No time to stand beneath the boughs
And stare as long as sheep or cows.

No time to see, when woods we pass,
Where squirrels hide their nuts in grass.

No time to see, in broad daylight,
Streams full of stars, like skies at night.

No time to turn at Beauty's glance,
And watch her feet, how they can dance.

No time to wait till her mouth can
Enrich that smile her eyes began.

A poor life this if, full of care,
We have no time to stand and stare.

W. H. Davies

Solitude is the profoundest fact of the human condition. Man is the only being who knows he is alone.

Octavio Paz

The most precious things in speech are pauses.

Ralph Richardson

My bed at night was under another haystack, where I rested comfortably, after having washed my blistered feet in a stream, and dressed them as well as I was able, with some cool leaves. When I took the road again next morning, I found that it lay through a succession of hop-grounds and orchards. It was sufficiently late in the year for the orchards to be ruddy with ripe apples; and in a few places the hop-pickers were already at work. I thought it all extremely beautiful, and made up my mind to sleep among the hops that night: imagining some cheerful companionship in the long perspective of poles, with the graceful leaves twining round them.

Charles Dickens

Silence is deep
as Eternity.

Thomas Carlyle

The love of learning,
   the sequestered nooks,
And all the sweet
   serenity of books.

Henry Wadsworth Longfellow

Once again
Do I behold these steep
  and lofty cliffs,
That on a wild secluded
  scene impress
Thoughts of more deep
  seclusion; and connect
The landscape with the
  quiet of the sky.

William Wordsworth

The game of draughts
we know is peculiarly
calculated to fix the
attention without
straining it. There is a
composure and
gravity in draughts
which insensibly
tranquillises the mind.

James Boswell

Be still, sad heart!
    And cease repining;
Behind the clouds
    is the sun still shining.

Henry Wadsworth Longfellow

Painting is silent poetry,
and poetry is a
speaking picture.

Simonides of Ceos

"Be quiet you young imps, you young scamps, you young ruffians; be quiet and walk across the room nicely; there's good children!" said the schoolmaster, and they went quietly to their places and calmed down, whereupon the schoolmaster stood up before them and said a short prayer.

Björnstjerne Björnson

An imperturbable demeanour comes from perfect patience. Quiet minds cannot be perplexed or frightened, but go on in fortune or misfortune at their own private pace, like a clock during a thunderstorm.

Robert Louis Stevenson

Let thy West Wind sleep on
The Lake; speak silence with
  thy glimmering eyes,
And wash the dusk with silver.

William Blake

… a great
sweet silence.

Henry James, Jr

Happy the man,
    whose wish and care
A few paternal acres bound,
Content to breathe his native air
In his own ground.

Alexander Pope

The fruitful ground, the quiet mind.

Henry Howard, Earl of Surrey

No foulness, nor
tumult, in those
tremulous streets,
that filled, or fell,
beneath the moon;
but rippled music
of majestic change,
or thrilling silence.

John Ruskin

Be still and
know that
I am God.

The Bible, Psalm 46

"I don't think" –
said Alice. "Then
you shouldn't talk,"
said the Hatter.

Lewis Carroll

47

It is a beauteous evening, calm and free,
The holy time is quiet as a Nun
Breathless with adoration: the broad sun
Is sinking down in its tranquility;
The gentleness of heaven broods o'er
    the Sea.

William Wordsworth

You tell me that silence
is nearer to peace than poems

Leonard Cohen

Children love to be
alone because alone
is where they know
themselves, and
where they dream.

Roger Rosenblatt

What I say is,
patience, and
shuffle the cards.

Cervantes

The love
The faith
The peace
Within us

Maori song

The sea is calm tonight.
The tide is full, the moon lies fair
Upon the straits; - on the French coast the light
Gleams and is gone; the cliffs of England stand,
Glimmering and vast, out in the tranquil bay.
Come to the window, sweet is the night air!
Only, from the long line of spray
Where the sea meets the moon-blanch'd land,
Listen! You hear the grating roar
Of pebbles which the waves draw back, and fling,
At their return, up the high strand,
Begin, and cease, and then again begin,
With tremulous cadence slow, and bring
The eternal note of sadness in.

Matthew Arnold

People say life is the thing,
but I prefer reading.

Logan Perasall Smith

Summer makes a silence
after spring.

Victoria Sackville-West

There are five stages of meditation.
The fifth meditation is the
meditation on serenity, in which
thou risest above love and hate,
tyranny and thraldom, wealth and
want, and regardest thine own fate
with impartial calmness and perfect
tranquillity.

Buddha

To break the stillness of the hour
  There is no sound, no voice, no stir;
  Only the croak of frogs,—the whirr
Of crickets hidden in leaf and flower.

Thomas Irwin

There was never a
child so lovely but
his mother was glad
to get him asleep.

Ralph Waldo Emerson

Simplicity and repose are the qualities that measure the true value of any work of art.

Frank Lloyd Wright

There was no-one to tell about it.
There was, perhaps, nothing to tell.
All the world we could see lay
motionless in the muted splendour
of the sunrise. Had we been able to
hear a bird calling from some pine-
tree, or sheep bleating in some
valley, the summit stillness would
have been familiar; now it was
different. It was as if the world had
held its breath for us… Trying to talk
about it… would have seemed
profane; if there was anything we
shared, it was the sudden sense of
quiet and rest.

David Roberts

There is a fellowship
more quiet even than
solitude, and which,
rightly understood, is
solitude made perfect.
To live out of doors with
the woman a man loves
is of all lives the most
complete and free.

Robert Louis Stevenson

Tired nature's
sweet restorer,
balmy sleep.

Edward Young

I leave this notice on my door
For each accustomed visitor:
'I am gone into the fields
To take what this sweet hour
    yields;
Reflection, you may come
    tomorrow…

Percy Bysshe Shelley

A happy family
is but an earlier
heaven.

Anonymous

I know of no quiet
quite like that of a
man's club at about half
past nine on a summer
Sunday evening.

John O'Hara

The real in
us is silent;
the acquired
is talkative.

Kahlil Gibran

No life, my honest scholar,
no life so happy and so
pleasant as the life of a
well-governed angle; for
when the lawyer is
swallowed up with business,
and the statesman is
preventing or contriving
plots, then we sit on
cowslip-banks, hear the
birds sing, and possess
ourselves in as much
quietness as these silent
silver streams, which we
now see glide so quietly
by us.

Izaak Walton

Solitude, though it may
be silent as light, is like
light, the mightiest of
agencies; for solitude is
essential to man. All men
come into this world
alone and leave it alone.

Thomas De Quincey

Happy are those who are still, and to whom things come.

Ben Okri

I must go down to the seas again, to
    the vagrant gypsy life,
To the gull's way and the whale's way,
    where the wind's like a whetted knife;
And all I ask is a merry yarn from a
    laughing fellow-rover,
And quiet sleep and a sweet dream
    when the long trick's over.

John Masefield

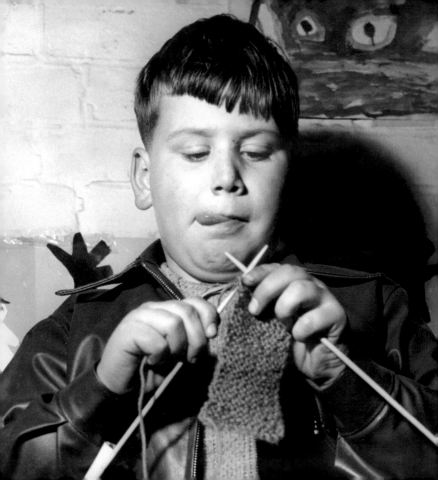

Study to be quiet and to do your own business, and to work with your own hands.

The Bible, 1 Thessalonians, 4:11

I would rather sit on a pumpkin, and have it all to myself, than be crowded on a velvet cushion.

Henry David Thoreau

...a well–spent day
brings happy sleep...

Leonardo da Vinci

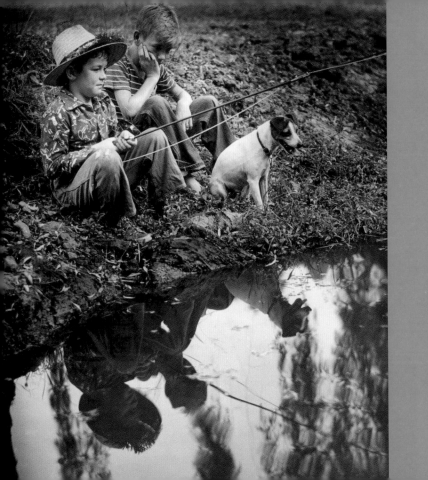

Oh, is the water sweet and cool,
Gentle and brown, above the pool?
And laughs the immortal river still
Under the mill, under the mill?
Say, is there Beauty yet to find?
And Certainty? and Quiet kind?
Deep meadows yet, for to forget
The lies, and truths, and pain?… oh! yet
Stands the Church clock at ten to three?
And is there honey still for tea?

Rupert Brooke

Youth is wholly experimental. The essence and charm of that unquiet and delightful epoch is ignorance of self as well as ignorance of life.

Robert Louis Stevenson

A room hung with pictures is a room hung with thoughts.

Joshua Reynolds

Give me the clear blue sky over my head, and the green turf beneath my feet, a winding road before me, and a three hours' march to dinner—and then to thinking! ...I begin to feel, think, and be myself again.

William Hazlitt

To see a World in a Grain of Sand
And a Heaven in a Wild Flower,
Hold Infinity in the palm of your hand
And Eternity in an hour.

William Blake

Picture Credits

All images Hulton Getty Picture Archive, unless otherwise stated.

Text Credits

Published by MQ Publications Limited
12 The Ivories, 6–8 Northampton Street, London N1 2HY
Tel: 020 7359 2244   Fax: 020 7359 1616
email: mail@mqpublications.com

Design: Bet Ayer
Series Editor: Tracy Hopkins

ISBN: 1 84072 390 4

Printed and bound in China